A Life of Grace for the Whole World

A Study Course on the House
of Bishops' Pastoral Teaching on
the Environment

**JERRY CAPPEL and
STEPHANIE M. JOHNSON**

Church Publishing
NEW YORK

Church Publishing
19 East 34th Street
New York, NY 10016
www.churchpublishing.org

Cover design by Jennifer Kopec, 2Pug Design
Typeset by Beth Oberholtzer

Library of Congress Cataloging-in-Publication Data
A record of this book is available from the Library of Congress.

ISBN-13: 978-0-8192-3380-6 (pbk.)
ISBN-13: 978-0-8192-3381-3 (ebook)

Printed in the United States of America

Contents

Welcome!

We're glad you're here! Together we will journey deeper into faith and an appreciation for God's great creation. In our five weeks together, you will learn much about your own life, the God you love, the earth, and all its creatures.

It all starts with a letter, one written by the bishops of the Episcopal Church. Do you know any bishops? All together, the bishops are called "the House of Bishops," and we find them around the world. The House of Bishops meets twice a year to consider issues of the church and pray for the people of the world. In 2011, they issued a pastoral teaching urging the church to deepen its concern and response to the environmental crisis as a response to God's love for all creation. It was the first ever teaching on the environment issued by the House of Bishops.

This pastoral teaching is the starting point for *A Life of Grace for the Whole World*.

What's our hope? Well, to quote the bishops in their letter, our goal is "to pay heed to the suffering of the earth. . . ." The bishops point out that "we are engaged in the process of destroying our very being. If we cannot live in harmony with the earth, we will not live in harmony with one another."

Wow! That's serious stuff.

The bishops also remind us that we can take action for creation *now*: "This is the appointed time for all God's children to work for the common goal of renewing the earth as a hospitable abode for the flourishing of all life."

They encourage the people of our church (including you!) to consider that "we are called to speak and act on behalf of God's good creation."

That's right. The bishops want *you* to speak and act on behalf of God's creation. Are you ready?

This may seem like a big and abstract concept, but this *Youth Booklet*, along with our five sessions together, will help you see how these ideas are actually relevant and timely in our lives today.

SESSION 1

A Time for Harmony with God's Creation

Opening Prayer

Creator, we give you thanks for all you are and all you bring to us for our visit within your creation. In Jesus, you place the Good News in the center of this sacred circle through which all of creation is related. You show us the way to live a generous and compassionate life. Give us your strength to live together with respect and commitment as we grow in your spirit for you are God, now and forever. Amen.*

Take Note

A Life of Grace for the Whole World is about deepening our relationship with God and creation. People often learn about the environment in school, but don't often talk about it in church. During

---

* www.episcopalchurch.org/library/document/gathering-prayer-bookmark

these sessions, we will explore and learn about why taking care of the earth is part of our faith life.

In our first session together, as we toured our church, we noted particular images of nature throughout the church and outside the building. This connection with nature makes sense because, throughout the Bible, stories are told about humanity's relationship with nature. Stories range from the parting of the Red Sea, to Moses climbing the mountaintop to hear God, to Jesus's parables about the nature of faith (which grows from a small mustard seed into flourishing life). Jesus preaches to thousands of people in the heart of nature—on the shore of the Sea of Galilee, on the plains, and from the mountain.

Throughout our time together, a "Tree of Life"—designed by the group—will be the central focus of our creative work as a visual symbol of harmony and healing of the earth.

Engage

Celebrating the beauty of God's creation is a way to deepen our appreciation of all that God loves. Often people write or draw to express these types of emotions, as illustrated by the psalms, which praise God for life and the beauty of the earth.

In the following space, either draw a picture of something in nature that gives you great joy in God *or* write a haiku[1] or poem about God's creation.

Reflect

In the book of Genesis (the first book in the Bible) we read that:

> *God made the wild animals of the earth of every kind, and the cattle of every kind, and everything that creeps upon the ground of every kind. And God saw that it was good. Then God said, "Let us make humankind in our image, according to our likeness; and let them have dominion over the fish of the sea, and over the birds of the air, and over the cattle, and over all the wild animals of the earth, and over every creeping thing that creeps upon the earth." (Gen. 1:25–26)*

---

1. Haikus are a Japanese way to write thoughts, traditionally about nature, in three short lines, with the rhythm of five syllables, seven syllables, and five syllables. Here is an example:

God's good earth is vast.
God's good earth is beautiful.
God's good earth is great.

Take a few minutes in silence. Then write a short prayer thanking God for all things in creation for which you are grateful. Then write another short prayer asking for God's wisdom in taking care of creation.

- Here's a start: Loving God, I am so thankful for . . .

_____

_____

_____

_____

_____

_____

_____

- Gracious God, guide me in the care of . . .

_____

_____

_____

_____

_____

_____

_____

_____

Respond

Here, in each session of this *Youth Booklet*, we will extend a weekly challenge.

This week we challenge you to spend 5–10 minutes outside at least once during the week. Do so without distractions, including technology (like phones, music, etc.).

Take a few minutes to write—in a short list or in sentences—the answers to the following questions:

- What did you hear?

_____

_____

_____

_____

_____

_____

_____

GOOD TO KNOW!

In 2016, twenty-one youth from the ages of 8–19, through the organization Our Children's Trust, filed a lawsuit against the federal government on the grounds that their lives were at risk from climate change.

- What did you see that you hadn't noticed before?

_____

_____

_____

_____

_____

- What did you smell?

_____

_____

_____

_____

_____

- How did you feel? (For example, did you feel calm in the outside world or anxious to be back with your technology or inside?)

_____

_____

_____

_____

_____

_____

- If you went outside more than once, did you notice different things the next time? If so, what were they?

_____

_____

_____

_____

_____

_____

Closing Prayer

Loving God, we are grateful for the wonder of creation and the many gifts you have given us. We recognize that the earth is suffering because of how we live and act. We ask that you give us energy and courage to respond in hope and faithfulness so that the face of the earth will be renewed for all generations. Amen.

SESSION 2

A Time for Care for the Whole Creation

Opening Prayer

We have forgotten who we are.
We have become separate from the movements of the earth.
We have turned our backs on the cycles of life.
We have forgotten who we are.

We have sought only our own security.
We have exploited simply for our own ends.
We have distorted our knowledge.
We have abused our power.
We have forgotten who we are.

Now the land is barren
And the waters are poisoned
And the air is polluted.
We have forgotten who we are.

Now the forests are dying
And the creatures are disappearing
And the humans are despairing.
We have forgotten who we are.

We ask forgiveness.
We ask for the gift of remembering,
We ask for the strength to change,
all for the love of our Creator. *Amen*.[2]

Take Note

Our conversation in session 1 explores how humanity relates to the rest of creation.

God's invitation to all is to care for creation, but sometime we have forgotten that invitation as we focus on ourselves, our families, and the people around us. This continued concern *primarily on human beings* has affected the world around us, contributing to the rapid increase of species extinction and the loss of habitats to support a thriving, bountiful natural system.

Our exploration in this session allows us to consider what a blessed creation God has made, to mourn that which has been lost, and to think about how we can care for all the creatures and land.

---

2. United Nations Environment Programme. "Only One Earth," a United Nations Environment Programme publication for Environmental Sabbath/Earth Rest Day, June 1990. UN Environment Programme, DC2-803, United Nations, New York, NY 10017. Used by permission.

Engage

In watching the clip from *The Lion King*, Simba looks into the water and sees his own image. In the background we hear the voice of Mufasa, Simba's dad, saying, "Simba, you have forgotten who you are."

In Genesis we learned that we are created in the image of God. As Christians we believe that the image that reflects back to us when we look in the mirror is the image of God. It's a concept which can be both challenging and exhilarating at the same time.

Go to a mirror in your house and look at your image for 30–45 seconds.

What was that experience like? Is it hard or easy to imagine that you are created in the image of God?

Next, look around for the next human you encounter. It might be a sibling, friend, or parent.

Are they all created in the image of God?

GOOD TO KNOW!

C. S. Lewis, the author of *The Chronicles of Narnia*, which was mentioned during the group session, created the book's main character—the lion Aslan— as a symbol of God's loving presence. Lewis was a well-known Christian theologian who wrote some of the most influential and important books on Christian life and living in the twentieth century.

Reflect

In the group session, we mourned for and acknowledged the extinction of several species as a way to recognize these species both by name and as living creatures of God's creation.

When a person dies, newspapers and social media often publish an obituary, which includes a summary of a person's life. Go online and research the species for which you lit a candle in the Cycle of Life. Find out about that species' habitat, when they lived, why they died, and so forth.

In the space below, write an obituary for that species.

_____

_____

_____

_____

_____

GOOD TO KNOW! In the book of Genesis there are two versions of the creation story. While there is a range of theories as to why this is, it is generally accepted by biblical scholars that each version was originally conceived and written by two different authors. The first account focuses on the creation of the entire cosmos (Gen. 1:1–2:3) and the second account focuses on the creation of humankind in the Garden of Eden (Gen. 2:4–25).

Respond

Here, in each session of this *Youth Booklet*, we will extend a weekly challenge.

In the week ahead, keep track of the animals, birds, and bugs in your neighborhood. If possible, use your phone to take some pictures or write a list on paper of the living creatures in the world around you. Consider keeping a running tally of all the animals you have noticed.

Write here the types of creatures you have seen:

_____

_____

_____

_____

_____

As you feel comfortable, when you encounter these creatures, offer a short, silent "Thank you God for this life."

How did it feel to offer a short word of gratitude to God for these creatures?

_____

_____

_____

_____

_____

Closing Prayer

Dear God, we know that after the great flood, you promised never again to flood the earth, and you sent a rainbow as a sign to show that this covenant was between you and every living creature. Now we make a covenant with you, with all living creatures today, and with those yet to be. We agree to try to care for all God's creation. We confess that we put creatures at the risk of death and extinction. We ask for your trust and as a symbol of our intention, we mark our covenant with you by adding the pictures of these extinct animals to our Tree of Life. This will be a sign of the covenant between ourselves and every living thing that was and is found on earth. Amen.

GOOD TO KNOW!

We cannot separate ourselves as humans from the rest of the created order. The creation story (in Genesis) presents the interdependence of all God's creatures in their wonderful diversity and fragility, and in their need of protection from dangers of many kinds.

—HOUSE OF BISHOPS' PASTORAL TEACHING

SESSION 3

A Time for Thirsting for Justice

Opening Prayer

Loving God, we thank you for the blessings of this life—our family and friends, our neighbors and those who teach us. We know that you invite us to care for all those who are in need. May we be mindful of those who are hungry or thirsty, those who do not have housing or a safe place to be. Give us courage and wisdom to make a difference in the lives of those who are suffering or in need. All this we ask in the name of your son, Jesus Christ. Amen.

Take Note

Many of the stories in the Bible have water as a central theme or focus. In part, this is because throughout time humans have recognized both their dependence on and the destructive force of water.

Water is a unifying blessing for all people and creatures. Without water, none of us will survive. As Christians we use water as a symbol of our entry into the life of the church, following on Jesus's baptism in the Jordan, where his divinity was fully revealed.

Together we explore our relationship with water to better understand our need to care for this resource and to help those who are without clean, sufficient water.

Engage

In the group session, we reviewed the prayers over the blessing of water during baptism and we discussed our Baptismal Covenant. The water of baptism reminds us of not only our human need for water but also our shared baptism into the life of Christ.

Ask your parent(s) and/or godparents to recall the day you were baptized. Talk with them about why they chose to baptize you. Ask them to show you pictures or other remembrances of your baptism.

GOOD TO KNOW!

According to the United Nations, an American uses on average 56,532 gallons of water per year. To get a sense of this, imagine over 50,000 gallons of milk containers in your house! By comparison, in Mali in West Africa, one of the hottest countries in the world, the average annual use is 1,056 per year.*

* www.unwater.org/downloads/Water_facts_and_trends.pdf

In the space below, write things that you learned about your baptism. Was there anything that surprised you about your baptism?

_____

_____

_____

_____

_____

If you are not baptized, talk with your parent(s) about their decision not to baptize you. Write in the space below your thoughts and ideas about not being baptized.

_____

_____

_____

_____

_____

Reflect

In the video, we saw young women walking miles to carry water to their families. In many cases, this is their primary job, which prevents them from playing, socializing, going to school, and getting an education. Much of their focus in on getting and carrying water.

To raise your awareness about the burden of water-bearing, for one day carry water with you everywhere. Fill a 16-oz. bottle of water to carry every place you go.

Unless you have no other access to water, do *not* drink this water but rather just feel the weight of it.

In the spaces below, answer the following questions:

• Did you forget the water? If so, how many times?

_____

_____

_____

_____

_____

• Were there times when the bottle felt heavy or burdensome? What were your thoughts when this happened?

_____

_____

_____

_____

_____

- Did you share with anyone that you were carrying water for a day as an attempt to better understand water scarcity?

_____

_____

_____

_____

_____

_____

_____

When your day is done, pour the water into the ground, returning it to the water cycle.

Respond

Here, in each session of this *Youth Booklet*, we will extend a weekly challenge.

Recognizing that water is both a sacred gift and for many an extremely limited resource, take time this week to be mindful of water in your daily life. Here are two options for this week's challenge:

- *Option 1:* Limit your showers to no more than five minutes. When you brush your teeth, don't let the water continue to run.

- *Option 2:* Express gratitude for water when you turn on the faucet by saying or silently praying these words: "Thank you, God, for the gift of water."

Depending on which option you choose (perhaps both?), answer the questions on the following pages.

GOOD TO KNOW!

The wealthier nations whose industries have exploited the environment seem to have forgotten that those who consume most of the world's resources also have contributed the most pollution to the world's rivers and oceans, have stripped the world's forests of healing trees, have destroyed both numerous species and their habitats, and have added the most poison to the earth's atmosphere.

—HOUSE OF BISHOPS' PASTORAL TEACHING

- Did five minutes seem like a long time or a short time for a shower? How long do you think your shower normally is?

_____

_____

_____

_____

_____

- How often did you remember to turn off the water when brushing your teeth?

_____

_____

_____

_____

_____

- When turning on faucets, how often did you remember to thank God for the gift of water? When you did remember, what difference did it make to you? For example, did it help you feel closer to God? Did it make you more grateful for the gift of water?

_____

_____

_____

_____

_____

_____

_____

- Describe your experience of thanking God for water.

_____

_____

_____

_____

_____

_____

_____

Closing Prayer
(from the Book of Common Prayer, p. 306)

We thank you, Almighty God, for the gift of water. Over it the Holy Spirit moved in the beginning of creation. Through it you led the children of Israel out of their bondage in Egypt into the land of promise. In it your Son Jesus received the Baptism of John and was anointed by the Holy Spirit as the Messiah, the Christ, to lead us, through his death and resurrection, from the bondage of sin into everlasting life. We thank you, Father, for the water of Baptism. In it we are buried with Christ in his death. By it we share in his resurrection. Through it we are reborn by the Holy Spirit. Amen.

SESSION 4

A Time to Renew Ancient Practices

Opening Prayer
(adapted from the UN Environmental Sabbath Service)

God beyond all sensation, we who have lost our sense and our senses—our touch, our smell, our vision of who we are; we who frantically force and press all things, without rest for body or spirit, hurting our earth and injuring ourselves: we call a halt. We want to rest. We need to rest and allow the earth to rest. We need to reflect and to rediscover the mystery of God, the wonderful expression of life, the source of the fascination that calls all things to communion with the Holy Spirit. We declare a Sabbath, a space of quiet: for simple being and let-ting be; for recovering the great, forgotten truths; for learning how to live again. Amen.[3]

---

3. United Nations Environment Programme. From "Only One Earth," a United Nations Environment Programme publication for Environmental Sabbath/Earth Rest Day, June 1990. UN Environment Programme, DC2-803, United Nations, New York, NY 10017. Used by permission.

Take Note

A spiritual practice is the way people of faith become alert and aware to God in their lives. Spiritual practices can include prayer, meditation, fasting, retreats away from daily life, journaling, and Sabbath-keeping.

Sabbath is often referred to as a day in the week, Sunday in the Christian calendar. But it can also be a stepping away from the busyness of life to encounter God in the world around us.

The idea of Sabbath occurs in many places in the Bible, including the story of God resting on the seventh day of creation.

Through Sabbath-keeping and fasting we have space in our mind and hearts to consider all of God's creation.

Engage

Silently re-read the opening prayer from this session, printed above.

- Make a list of all the things that you are "frantically pressing forward on":

_____

_____

_____

_____

_____

_____

- Next, write down what a quiet day (with no chores, work, sports, after-school activities, school, etc.) could look like. Note specific things that would make you happy and joyful on this imaginary Sabbath day, for example bike-riding, hiking, reading, drawing, and so on:

_____

_____

_____

_____

_____

_____

- Finally, write down things in your life that you wish you no longer had on your schedule (even though they may still need to remain in your life for practical and important reasons):

_____

_____

_____

_____

_____

_____

If you eliminated some of the busyness from your life, how might you feel in the silence? What might stillness be like?

_____

_____

_____

_____

_____

In the silence, what words of prayer might you lift to God? Write them here:

_____

_____

_____

_____

_____

With the possibility of more space in your life, who would you like to spend more time with? What places might you like to visit?

_____

_____

_____

_____

_____

What prevents you from spending time with people you care for or in places that are important to you?

_____

_____

_____

_____

_____

_____

_____

Reflect

One area in our lives that takes a lot of our energy is maintaining our possessions. While it is totally normal to want to have trendy clothes and the newest technology, sometimes we have more than we need.

GOOD TO KNOW!

According to the American Academy of Pediatrics, the average American child/youth spends seven hours a day viewing and using an electronic device such as a computer, TV, tablet, or smart phone.*

_____

* "Media and Children Communication Toolkit," American Academy of Pediatrics, 2016. www.aap.org/en-us/advocacy-and-policy/aap-health-initiatives

If you could own only fifty possessions, what would they be? List them here.

_____

_____

_____

_____

_____

_____

_____

_____

_____

_____

_____

_____

_____

_____

_____

_____

After you've completed this list of fifty items, what things were or were not on the list that surprised you?

_____

_____

_____

_____

_____

_____

Respond

Here in this *Youth Booklet*, in each session we offer you a weekly challenge.

Our lives are filled not only with taking care of many things but also with the busyness of social media and screen time (TV, phone, tablet, computer, etc.). In this week's challenge, we invite you to step back from *one* of these distractions. Here are some options to consider:

Option 1:

Take Sabbath time away from at least *one* type of social media for a day, using that time to engage in some other activity that connects with God, people, or nature. After doing this, reflect on the experience:

- What did it feel like to be away from social media?

_____

_____

_____

_____

_____

- If you spent the free time in nature, were you able to—as the bishops' pastoral teaching says—"savor the grace of creation"? In other words, did you experience peace, joy, and a sense of awe while outside?

_____

_____

_____

_____

_____

GOOD TO KNOW!

Sabbath requires rest, that we might remember our rightful place as God's creatures in relationship with every other creature of God. Sabbath rest requires humans to live lightly on the face of the earth, neither to expend energy nor to consume it, not to work for gain alone, but to savor the grace of creation.

—HOUSE OF BISHOPS' PASTORAL TEACHING

- Did you connect with people in a different way than you expected? If so, how?

_____

_____

_____

_____

_____

Option 2:

Try fasting from shopping for the week—don't buy clothes, don't invest in any technology, instead of going to a movie, get together with friends to play games, hike, or cook together. If you must spend something, only buy absolute necessities, like groceries.

- How did it feel to take a break from spending? How challenging was it?

_____

_____

_____

_____

_____

_____

- How did it feel to "step out of" the mainstream of culture, where spending money is a daily activity for most people?

_____

_____

_____

_____

_____

- Were there times when friends or family members thought you were odd for doing this? How did you respond?

_____

_____

_____

_____

_____

Option 3:

Clean out your room of things which aren't used or worn regularly and donate these items to charity.

- What does it feel like to get rid of things you no longer use or need?

_____

_____

_____

_____

_____

- How difficult was it to make decisions about what to give away and what to keep?

_____

_____

_____

_____

- If you donated your goods to a charity, did you pick a specific one? If so, how did you choose?

_____

_____

_____

_____

_____

Closing Prayer

(from the Book of Common Prayer, p. 825)

> *O God, in the course of this busy life, give us times of refreshment and peace; and grant that we may so use our leisure to rebuild our bodies and renew our minds, that our spirits may be opened to the goodness of your creation; through Jesus Christ our Lord.* Amen.

A Time to Commit and Act

Opening Prayer

(From the Book of Common Prayer, p. 827)

> *Almighty and everlasting God, you made the universe with all its marvelous order, its atoms, worlds, and galaxies, and the infinite complexity of living creatures: Grant that, as we probe the mysteries of your creation, we may come to know you more truly, and more surely fulfill our role in your eternal purpose; in the name of Jesus Christ our Lord. Amen.*

Take Note

Throughout our study of *A Life of Grace*, you reflected on your relationship to God and to God's creation. You also examined the link between you and the larger world. In our final session together, we invite to consider how you can care for all creation—in your community, congregation, and the world. The constant theme for each session has been *time*—a time for *harmony*, a time to *care for creation*, a time to *renew our hearts*, a time to *thirst for justice*, and a time to *act*.

While *our* time can seem both limitless (because of the promise of the future) and limited (because sometimes we have too much to do), *God's* time is never ending. In this final session, we invite you to consider your time on this earth *today* . . . and into the *future*.

Engage

- Imagine yourself ten years from now. How old will you be? Imagine what you might be doing and where you might be living.

_____

_____

_____

_____

_____

_____

- Now write a letter to yourself broadly describing what has happened to you from today through the next ten years. Speak about how you've been a leader in your congregation, community, region, and the world on issues that matter to you. Note how the environment has or has not improved. Talk about what specific actions you took to make a difference by living lightly on God's earth. As a reminder that you, a beloved child of God, is created in God's image, sign the letter with a closing such as "Beloved in Christ Jesus" or "Beloved Child of God."

Dear me . . .

_____

_____

_____

_____

_____

_____

_____

_____

GOOD TO KNOW!

The Marshall Islands, home to Kathy Keyner, is one of the most geographically isolated island chains in the world. It is at high risk of significant flooding from rising waters resulting from climate change. Climatologists suggest that the Marshall Islands— along with other island nations—may actually need to be abandoned and the entire population moved to new countries.

Reflect

Over the course of this program, we have together designed and decorated a Tree of Life to celebrate and reflect the shared joy, beauty, and bounty of God's creation. In the space below, sketch out your own Tree of Life. Either draw pictures of or write the names of creatures, pets, things, people, and places in nature that are important and sacred to you.

GOOD TO KNOW!

In assuming with new vigor our teaching office, we, your bishops, commit ourselves to a renewal of these spiritual practices in our own lives, and invite you to join us in this commitment for the good of our souls and the life of the world. Moreover, in order to honor the goodness and sacredness of God's creation, we, as brothers and sisters in Christ, commit ourselves to act.

—HOUSE OF BISHOPS' PASTORAL TEACHING

Respond

Put the date on the Tree of Life you drew above. Place this booklet someplace where you can find it in a year. On your phone calendar, paper calendar, or computer calendar, set a reminder to look at your Tree of Life and your Letter to Yourself one year from today's date.

Closing Prayer

Gracious God, bless us with words to speak on behalf of creation for us and for future generations. Creator God, bless us with strong and compassionate hearts to feel the sadness and pain of all who suffer from environmental decay. Loving God, give us eyes to see and celebrate the beauty in all that you have created. Amen.